AUTUMN

SEASONS OF THE YEAR

By Harriet Brundle

SEASONS OF THE YEAR

©2016
Book Life
King's Lynn
Norfolk
PE30 4LS

ISBN: 978-1-910512-56-2

Written by:
Harriet Brundle

Edited by:
Gemma McMullen

Designed by:
Ian McMullen

A catalogue record for this book
is available from the British Library.

Contents

Words that appear like **this** can be *found* in the glossary on page 24.

Seasons of the Year

There are four seasons in a year. The seasons are called Spring, Summer, Autumn and Winter.

Every season is different.
This book is about Autumn!

Autumn

Autumn happens after Summer and before Winter. The Autumn months are September, October and November.

January

Sun	Mon	Tue	Wed	Thu	Fri	Sat
1	2	3	4	5	6	7
8	9	10	11	12	13	14
15	16	17	18	19	20	21
22	23	24	25	26	27	28
29	30	31				

February

Sun	Mon	Tue	Wed	Thu	Fri	Sat
			1	2	3	4
5	6	7	8	9	10	11
12	13	14	15	16	17	18
19	20	21	22	23	24	25
26	27	28	29			

March

Sun	Mon	Tue	Wed	Thu	Fri	Sat
			1	2	3	
4	5	6	7	8	9	10
11	12	13	14	15	16	17
18	19	20	21	22	23	24
25	26	27	28	29	30	31

April

Sun	Mon	Tue	Wed	Thu	Fri	Sat
1	2	3	4	5	6	7
8	9	10	11	12	13	14
15	16	17	18	19	20	21
22	23	24	25	26	27	28
29	30					

May

Sun	Mon	Tue	Wed	Thu	Fri	Sat
		1	2	3	4	5
6	7	8	9	10	11	12
13	14	15	16	17	18	19
20	21	22	23	24	25	26
27	28	29	30	31		

June

Sun	Mon	Tue	Wed	Thu	Fri	Sat
				1	2	
3	4	5	6	7	8	9
10	11	12	13	14	15	16
17	18	19	20	21	22	23
24	25	26	27	28	29	30

July

Sun	Mon	Tue	Wed	Thu	Fri	Sat
1	2	3	4	5	6	7
8	9	10	11	12	13	14
15	16	17	18	19	20	21
22	23	24	25	26	27	28
29	30	31				

August

Sun	Mon	Tue	Wed	Thu	Fri	Sat
		1	2	3	4	
5	6	7	8	9	10	11
12	13	14	15	16	17	18
19	20	21	22	23	24	25
26	27	28	29	30	31	

September

Sun	Mon	Tue	Wed	Thu	Fri	Sat
						1
2	3	4	5	6	7	8
9	10	11	12	13	14	15
16	17	18	19	20	21	22
23	24	25	26	27	28	29
30						

October

Sun	Mon	Tue	Wed	Thu	Fri	Sat

November

Sun	Mon	Tue	Wed	Thu	Fri	Sat

December

Sun	Mon	Tue	Wed	Thu	Fri	Sat

Autum

The daytime feels shorter in Autumn than in Summer. This is because there are less hours of sunlight.

The Weather

The weather starts to get colder in Autumn. There is often rain and wind.

It can be foggy in Autumn. The fog makes it hard for us to see.

Animals

Animals must eat lots in Autumn to prepare for the cold Winter.

Animals need fat on their bodies to keep warm.

On a cold Autumn morning, look out for spiders in their webs.

Spider

Web

Plants

There are lots of berries on the bushes in Autumn.

Be careful! Not all berries are safe for us to eat.

Conker

Horse chestnut trees grow
conkers in the Autumn.
The brown conkers grow
inside a prickly case.

In the Garden

The leaves on the trees go brown and red.
They fall from the trees onto the ground.

Summer

Autumn

As the weather gets colder, the Summer plants start to die and the garden changes colour.

Food

Pumpkin

Pumpkins grow in Autumn. We can use them to make pumpkin soup.

Which of these have you seen before?

Carrot

Beetroot

Root vegetables are ready to be eaten in Autumn.

What do we Wear in Autumn?

We may need our coats in Autumn so we can stay warm if the weather is cold.

Coat

Don't forget your boots if it is raining!

Wellington boots stop our feet getting wet.

Things to do in Autumn

In Autumn we celebrate Harvest Festival. Food is sent to those less *fortunate* than us.

It is fun to pick the last of the apples left on the trees in Autumn.

We can use them to make apple pie!

Fun in Autumn

Look at the leaves on the trees and on the ground. How many different colours can you see?

In America, the
Autumn season
is called Fall.

23

Glossary

Foggy: when a thick cloud of water hangs in the air making it hard for us to see.

Fortunate: when something is good or lucky.

Root Vegetables: a type of vegetable which grows underneath the soil.

Index